Nijo Castle

World Heritage

Eastern aerial view of Nijo Castle in its entirety

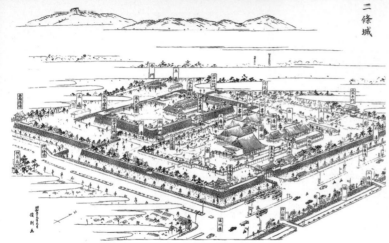

二條城

Picture by Toshinori Takemura

Past and Present
── Included Five-Story Tower when Originally Built

Once a graceful, dignified tower five stories high stood in Nijo Castle, which the shogun Tokugawa Ieyasu had built in 1602. We can still see how it appeared and was situated by looking at the folding screen painting of the period, entitled "Sights in and around Kyoto" (Shoko-ji Temple, Takaoka City). The castle's tall donjon must have seemed to be glaring down upon the city of Kyoto, the symbol of a power which easily surpassed the Emperor's.

The Ninomaru Palace had been built first, and about twenty years later the Honmaru Palace was added. These palace complexes created the castle precincts' dimensions and convex layout, which remain to the present day. Nowadays, however, with the lofty tower gone, one has the sense of visiting a samurai's vast grand mansion more than a castle.

One distinct feature of Nijo Castle is the bright impression its exterior creates, which is not generally found in castles built upon hilltops.

Temporary Honmaru Palace in late Edo Period   (*Property of Tojo Museum of History*)

This old photograph, discovered in 1993 in the Tokugawa household, is an inestimable image showing the history of the castle. Shogun Yoshinobu Tokugawa's accommodation is depicted on the left side.

The present-day Honmaru Palace

Honmaru Palace was built by the third shogun Iemitsu. The original palace and tower, protected by the inner moat, were destroyed by fire in the Edo period (1603 - 1867), and the current palace – a valuable example of palace construction – is the former Katsura Imperial Family Palace moved here from the Kyoto Imperial Palace in the middle of the Meiji period (1868 - 1912).

往時と現在

Left Section of Folding Screen Depicting Kyoto Environs *(Property of Bukkyo University)*

This folding screen was brought back to Japan from the USA in recent times. It depicts Emperor Gomizuno-o's cavalcade entering Nijo Castle. The castle was at its most complete around the time of the Emperor's visit in 1626. Center is the Great East Gate (Higashi-Ote-Mon), to its left and right are the North and South corner turrets, and going back from the main gate we have the Ninomaru complex and beyond that the Honmaru complex, with the grand tower standing out. The main gate – with ox carts and samurai warriors congregated in front – extended out to the perimeter provided by Horikawa River (canal).

Retired shogun Hidetada and his son shogun Iemitsu lavishly entertained the Emperor, his wife (Hidetada's daughter) and other guests for five days. The Emperor even climbed the tower to view Kyoto. The illustration below depicts the bridge corridor that spanned the inner moat to connect the Ninomaru complex and the Honmaru complex.

Present-day Hommaru lookout gate

Illustration of replica of bridge corridor

Reconstruction of the Bridge Corridor
(Reconstructed by Asae Ozawa)

The lookout gate and East Bridge still remain on the inner moat on the east side of the Honmaru complex; however, in olden times, a two-tier corridor (bridge and overhead corridor) joined the Honmaru Palace to the Ninomaru palace. Honmaru's foundations stand higher than those of Ninomaru, and the corridor led from Honmaru's Tozamurai (Retainers Rooms) to the second floor of the lookout gate, then on eastward across the inner moat as the bridge corridor, and into the Tamarigura (storehouse). From here, a descent to the first floor was made where a corridor continued on to Ninomaru's Kuro-Shoin (inner audience chamber).

往時と現在

Ninomaru Palace Complex

Sole Remaining Architecture from Early Years of Edo Period

The sole remnant of the early Edo period found within Nijo Castle is the Ninomaru Palace complex (a national treasure). Covering more than 30,000 square meters, the site is surrounded by a thick wall, within which is a compound of linked palace buildings that draw backward in the form of a line of flying wild geese. These include Tozamurai, Shikidai, Ohiroma, Kuro-shoin and Shiro-shoin. Each is built in the shoin-zukuri style of construction developed for samurai residences in the Muromachi period, a style which was later firmly established in the Edo period. Although all of these structures today have clay-tiled roofs, when they were first built a different material was used, known as kokerabuki. This consisted of overlapping thin wood shavings produced by a carpenter's plane. It is likely, then, that these original roofs did not arouse the same overpowering sense one feels today. Given that the palace complexes within Edo Castle and Osaka Castle have both been lost, the scholarly value of the Ninomaru Palace complex is very high. Nevertheless, since reconstruction and renovations were carried out in subsequent eras, the compound's present form is not the same as the original. Still, the interior wall paintings which one finds in various rooms here, by artists of the Kano school, are precious examples of fine art in early modern times.

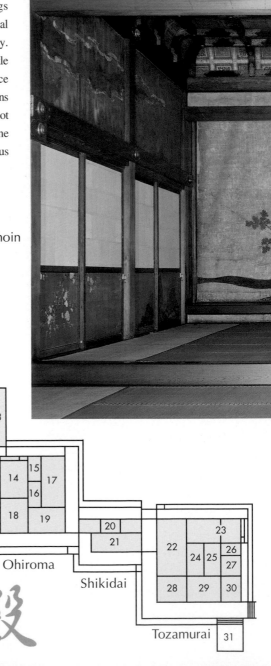

1	Ichinoma	17	Yonnoma
2	Cho-dainoma	18	Ninoma
3	Yonnoma	19	Sannoma
4	Ninoma	20	Roujyu-noma
5	Sannoma	21	Shikidainoma
6	Sashidenoma	22	Ichinoma
7	Ichinoma	23	Chokushinoma
8	Cho-dainoma	24	Store
9	Yonnoma	25	Fuyounoma
10	Ninoma	26	Cho-dainoma
11	Sannoma	27	Wakamatsunoma
12	Botannoma	28	Ninoma
13	Sotetsunoma	29	Sannoma
14	Ichinoma	30	Yanaginoma
15	Cho-dainoma	31	Kurumayose
16	Nando		

二の丸御殿

6

Tozamurai

Composed of eight chambers, Tozamurai is the largest building in the Ninomaru Palace complex. In this type of facility rooms were usually allotted to the shogun's retainers; in Nijo Castle, however, some were also used as waiting lounges for the daimyo, or feudal lords. Tozamurai is considered the final example of a medieval-style gathering place for samurai warriors. Its main chamber, Chokushinoma, situated in the northeast corner, was used as a waiting area for the Imperial Messenger prior to his meetings with the shogun. The room has a split-level floor which divides it into two sections. The upper level, stately in design, features a tokonoma, or raised decorative alcove, with staggered shelves, as well as ornamented doors known as chodaigamae. The wall paintings in the room depict maple trees, birds and flowers, and Japanese cypresses. Moving counterclockwise, the Chokushinoma gives way to the Ichinoma (First Room), Ninoma (Second Room), Sannoma (Third Room), and so on. These three rooms are each also known by the name Toranoma (Tiger Room), for their sliding panels are painted with images of tigers, bamboo and leopards. Placing such likenesses of tigers within sight of a hall's entryway was, during this period, an essential display of authority.

Maple Tree Images in Raised Level of Chokushinoma

(Messenger's Room)

This room, with 21-mat raised area and 35-mat lower area, was used by messengers of the Imperial court. At the far end of the room, on the left, is the tokonoma (large alcove), and to the right ornate, staggered shelves. On the right, there are ornate doors known as chodaigamae, and sliding doors to the left where the normally incorporated study space (stukeshoin) is absent. The picture on the paper sliding doors are of maple trees and a small island.

Staggered shelves (chigai-dana) in Upper Level of Imperial Messenger's Room

The fascia of the shelves, the bottom of the storage closets above the shelved alcove and the small strut with chamfered corners (ebizuka) are decorated with metal fittings (chirashikanagu). Each of the small sliding doors of the closet above the alcove depict from right a sprig of ume (Japanese apricot), Japanese rose, cherry and peony. Even the reverse sides of the sliding doors - that have no need of pictures - depict dandelions and violets.

遠
侍

Japanese Cypress in Lower Level of Imperial Messenger's Room

This is the picture on the panels on the south side of the room. A cypress grove is depicted on a golden background with gold clouds (genjigumo) trailing near and far, through the stout trees and spreading up to the top horizontal beam to convey a neat and powerful composition.

遠
侍

Bamboo Grove and Tigers in Second Room   *(Ninoma)*

In this room, one finds a linked composition on the north-and-east facing sliding doors. Here, against a golden background, tigers and leopards mingle at the water's edge in a bamboo grove. On the door left of center, a fierce tiger leisurely drinks while a leopard nestles up to it.

Ceiling Painting in Fifth Room
(Gonoma)

The entire ceiling flourishes with spreading grape vines, and the golden background glints like sunrays. This skillful composition depicts the boxed sections of the coffered ceiling as a grapevine trellis. The ornate metal fittings with the Tokugawa hollyhock family crest in the center fitted to the joints pull the "trellis" into focus.

Tiger in Bamboo Grove in Third Room
(Sannoma)

This depicts a leopard looking back at a tiger as it cuts through a bamboo grove on a golden background. The many tigers and leopards painted in the Tiger Room (Toranoma) express a gender representation of the Edo period, in which the tiger represents the male and the leopard the female.

Shikidai

Leaving Tozamurai from the western exit, one enters Shikidai, another hall for the shogun's retainers. Here were stationed the high-ranking roju, or councilors of the shogun's military government (bakufu), who accompanied the general during his stays in Kyoto. Shikidainoma is the long, rectangular-shaped antechamber; behind it one finds three smaller stations. The term shikidai means both greetings and gifts. Therefore, feudal lords paying social calls to the general would offer their salutations and gifts to the councilors here, who would in turn convey them to the shogun. Wall paintings in the Shikidainoma portray large, ancient pine trees extending their branches nearly to the ceiling. Among the imagery depicted in the three back rooms are wild geese and snowy herons.

Second Councilor's Station

This fixed picture on the five outward-looking panels handle the theme of pine trees. A golden background is home to two grand, ancient pines that spread up beyond the horizontal beam to present a colossal composition that is the start of the pine scene in the Grand Chambers (Ohiroma). This painting is said to be the work of Tanyu Kano.

Wild Geese in Rice Field in Ministers' Offices   *(Rojunoma)*

This is a linked composition on the east-and-west sliding doors. The scene, set on a golden background, is one of wild geese – some feeding on fallen grain in freshly harvested rice fields and some playing at the reedy water's edge – in an autumn countryside setting that imparts a sense of tranquility.

Painting of Herons on a Snowy Willow Tree in Third Councilor's Station *(Rojunoma)*

This picture exudes a sense of transition, depicting a golden background with three herons lingering on the bough of a snowy, ancient willow while to the left a fourth heron is in flight.

Councilor' Stations *(Rojunoma)*

These are the offices where the councilors attended to affairs. Here, the enclosing wall paintings have been prudently configured below the architectural border of the horizontal beams. From right to left, the first office depicts "spring & summer", the second "autumn" and the third "winter".

Ohiroma

Northwest of the Shikidai, one comes to the Ohiroma, a vast, tile-roofed building in the irimoya style. This was a hall of great public importance, for here the shogun himself would personally meet with groups of feudal lords. The building is surrounded by an engawa corridor. Ichinoma, the shogun's main, raised-level chamber, and Ninoma, where feudal lords would sit in obeisance, together comprise 92 tatami mats. Counterclockwise from here one finds Sannoma, followed by Yonnoma, also called Yarinoma (Spear Room) because armed bodyguards were concealed here. The shogun's elevated Ichinoma contains a raised alcove with staggered shelves

Ichinoma   *(Elevated Section)*

The two sections of the Ichinoma chamber are divided by a lacquered frame and a narrow wall between the frame and ceiling. The elevated section has a large, raised alcove and staggered shelves. On the right wall are the ornamental chodaigamae doors and on the left wall the built-in table or writing space (tsukeshoin). The ceiling is

as well as a writing or desk alcove and decorative chodaiga-mae doors, all rendered in the palatial shoin style. Its coffered ceiling is also built of two levels; the shogun would be seated beneath the higher portion. Venerable pine trees and birds of prey are painted on the walls in such a manner as to vigorously extend above and beyond the chamber's wooden beams, creating an air of forcefulness.

External Appearance

This is a southern view of the Ohiroma hall with the Ninomaru Garden off to the west. Kuro-shoin hall can be seen in the background on the left hand side. These two halls were built in a V-formation like that of geese in flight to afford from both a view of the Ninomaru garden. Back when the castle was in use, a Noh stage stood in front for the shogun and guests such as the Emperor to watch Noh dramas from the Ohimaru hall.

built to two heights; the shogun would sit under the higher (concave) part.

Garden   When the paper sliding doors are opened, a sweeping view of the garden unfurls, in which the trees are masterfully integrated with the pines depicted on the interior partitions and walls. Originally, the rear of the garden was occupied by a tower, or donjon, from which to the south side could be seen the hall to welcome the Emperor.

大
広
間

An Audience with the Shogun in Ichinoma and Ninoma

This scene reproduces an audience with the shogun, in which the shogun sits in the center of the elevated section with a pageboy sword bearer to his right; in the lower section to the right are ministers; to the left the ministers of the shogun, and then in the foreground the feudal lords strike dignified poses befitting such an audience. This is where the last Tokugawa shogun, Yoshinobu, announced the restoration of Imperial rule.

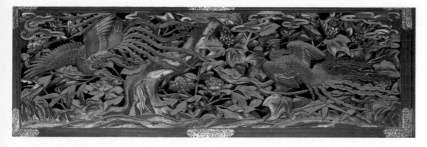

Carved Transom Screen on right side of Ninoma

This carving – in sharp contrast to the wall painting design – decorates the entire area between the horizontal beams. The delicately round-carved work (for viewing from both sides) suggests the nobility and wealth of the shogun. Both front and back are brilliantly colored without seeming gaudy.

Painting of Pine Tree and Peacocks in Ninoma

The patterned coffered ceiling and the metal fittings of the horizontal beams exalt the vividness of the room, while the giant pine, spreading across the upper and lower panels, and peacocks combine to offer a tranquil setting incorporating sliding doors that herald the Sannoma room. Above the first horizontal beam can be seen the exquisitely carved transom screens (ranma) depicting mythical phoenix birds in flight, which convey a sense of freedom.

Pine Tree and Peacock   This shows nearly all the partially shown picture at bottom right. The giant pine stretches low from left to right with a peacock in dignified pose standing to the left.

Painting of Pine Tree and Peacock in Sannoma

Below the flat, coffered ceiling unfolds the picture of a pine tree and peacock on a golden background. The photograph only shows part of the picture, the north-facing wall and four sliding doors that lead into the yonnoma. Above the doors is one of the elegantly decorated openwork transom screens replete with renowned round-carved, vividly colored peacocks, pine tree and peonies.

Painting of Pine Tree and Hawks in Yonnoma

At 55.5 mats, this is the biggest room in the Ohiroma chamber. The illustration of a giant pine and goshawks staring down at prey in the stream below gives this room an overall impression of fluidity. The transom screens are carved with pine trees, peonies and herbaceous peonies in a style of openwork that does not reveal the peacocks on the front sides of the carved screens.

Kuro-shoin

Passing through the wooden, corridor-like chamber known as Sotetsunoma, one enters Kuro-shoin. Built in the same tile-roofed irimoya style as Ohiroma, and also known as Shohiroma, or small hall, this served as the shogun's private meeting quarters. Its first chamber is smaller than the second but has two sets of staggered shelves joined in the right cor-ner. This feature is actually a characteristic of the Shiro-shoin found within the Honmaru at Osaka Castle which, like Nijo Castle's Kuro-shoin, was built under the supervision of Kobori Enshu (1579-1647). A tea master, architect, garden designer, calligrapher and poet, Kobori was a leader of early Edo culture. The wall paintings in the Kuro-shoin's first chamber depict red plum blossoms as well as an ancient pine tree rising above a brushwood fence; in the second room we encounter an eightfold blossoming cherry tree (yaezakura).

黒書院

Ichinoma and Ninoma

Although on a smaller scale than Ohiroma, Kuro-shoin (also known as Shohiroma) too is rendered in the palatial shoin style. It was used for state affairs and private meetings. This hall offered a backdrop of fluttering petals, frolicking waterfowl and running water that afforded the right atmosphere for talks between the shogun and his inner circle.

Pheasants under Cherry Tree in Ninoma

Here we have a charming early work by Naonobu Kano depicting a pair of pheasants and some small birds around a gorgeously radiant yaezakura cherry tree in proud bloom behind wicker and bamboo fencing.

Painting of Pheasant under Cherry Tree on Ornamental Doors of Ichinoma
(Elevated Section)

The painting on the ornamental chodaigamae doors depicts a soothing scene of a blossoming yaezakura cherry tree spreading up above the horizontal beams, with pheasant and azaleas at waters edge.

黒書院

Writing Alcove (Tsukeshoin) in Ichinoma

In this raised writing alcove we find a painted landscape composed by combining a multistory tower with natural scenery (roukaku-sansui) on paper sliding doors with lattice wainscoting (koshishoji). On adjacent sliding doors a red Japanese apricot tree (ume) and to its rear cherry blossoms and a woven brushwood fence offer a scene redolent of the changing seasons.

Shiro-shoin

This innermost building of the Ninomaru Palace complex, also known as Gozanoma, was used as the shogun's sitting room and bedroom. In the first chamber, following the principles of shoin-zukuri, are a decorative alcove, staggered shelves and ornamented doors. The atmosphere, however, is comparatively restrained and serene, for the Shiro-shoin was not a place for displaying the prestige and authority of the Tokugawa family but rather a private setting for their relaxation. The wall paintings are water and mountain landscapes with flowers and birds, brushed delicately in simple colors, not the dazzling gold-and-jasper found elsewhere in the palace. It is believed that the materials and styles used for paintings depended upon the function and social status of a room. It also seems that the design of this room was altered in the first half of the seventeenth century.

View of Ichinoma from Ninoma
(photo provided by Benrido)

Like the other halls, this room has the formal features collectively known as zashiki-kazari; however, the decorations are soothing Indian ink paintings. In sharp contrast, the 52 panels on the ceiling depict attractive seasonal wild flowers in rich hues - a fitting overhead view in the shogun's bedroom.

白書院

Landscape Painting in Raised Alcove of Ichinoma

This picture – part of the landscapes going from Ichinoma to Sannoma – depicts in detail a Chinese lake scene. The Kano brothers, Tanyu and Naonobu, painted this momentous work, which seems to resonate with the tête-à-tête of the elders and the creak of rowing in the tranquil snowy scene set off by a shore-side summerhouse and ancient tree.

Staggered Shelves in Ichinoma

To the right of the main raised alcove is the staggered-shelves alcove built in the same style as those in the other halls. Depicted here are multistory tower and farmhouse in an early spring scene. The small sliding doors of the cupboard are painted with fringed pink flowers and reverse sides depict sprigs of loquat, myrica and peach.

Ornamented Doors in Ichinoma

A bustling port scene on a tranquil, early spring day depicting buildings and workers unloading moored sailing boats. Behind these doors is a six-mat room (chodainoma) used for sleeping which is decorated with painting of autumn foliage.

Doors on Westside of Ninoma

Here we have a lightly colored landscape covering all the doors. This meticulously detailed picture shows a lake area in the foreground and mountains far off in the distance – a poetical piece revealing the genius of the artist.

Ninomaru Gardens

Isle of Eternal Youth (Shinsen-horai) fashioned by Enshu

In this strolling garden designed by Kobori Enshu, it is supposed that the world of the Isle of Eternal Youth has been expressed. In the center of the pond one finds Mt. Horai, where there lived a legendary hermit with miraculous powers. Crane Island and Turtle Island are seen to the mountain's right and left, respectively, along with four bridges and a waterfall set in the northwest corner. Along the pond's meandering shoreline, rocks and boulders of richly varied colors and shapes are arranged in beautifully complex combinations. When this garden was first laid out, the most exquisite viewpoint was from Ohiroma, but when Emperor Gomizuno-o came to visit, an imperial guest house was built for him south of the pond (it no longer stands), and the garden was redesigned to look its finest from there. In more recent years plum, cherry and camellia trees have been planted, adding seasonal coloring. Seiryuen, just north of the main Ninomaru Gardens, was completed in 1965, when trees, rocks, and a part of the mansion of wealthy merchant Suminokura Ryoui were relocated to these grounds. Its eastern side consists mostly of a lawn and deciduous trees in the manner of Western gardens. To the west, one strolls through a pond garden with two teahouses, Kountei and Warakuan.

二の丸
庭園

This pond strolling garden is said to have been designed by Kobori Enshu. Pond water runs south from the northwest cascades. Richly colored rocks, great and small, dominate the vista. In the center of the pond, one finds Mt. Horai, to its left Crane Island, and to its right Turtle Island.

Daidokoro

Standing separately to the east of the complex of buildings described above is the Daidokoro, comprised of two connected rooms, the Main Kitchen and Kitchen. The larger facility, on the north side, was where food was dished up for table settings, while actual cooking was done in the smaller south kitchen. Here the roof opens into a kind of chimney for releasing smoke from the fires. Although it is called a kitchen, this building's interior and exterior were both designed with a dignified beauty, and its total area covers 700 square meters. It is said that during the Kan'ei era (1622-44) many buildings for attendants stood west of the kitchen. Today, the Daidokoro stands alone and speaks to us of a style of life that was lived in samurai residences of that long ago era.

Full View of Daidokoro *(Kitchen)*

A wooden floor fans out to the southwest from the interior earth floor and a mezzanine has been built south of the entrance to accommodate a lookout post. In the west and south of the wooden-floored section there are shelves, cupboards and serving area, and to the southeast, a large corridor leads to the cookhouse kitchen.

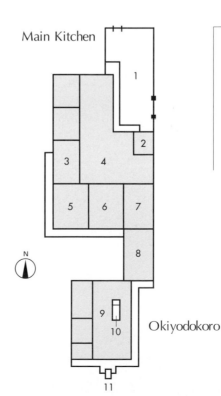

Main Kitchen

1	Doma
2	Miharidai
3	Gozendokoro
4	Gozendokoro-hikaenoma
5	Irorinoma
6	Tsunoma
7	Ichinoma
8	Ichinoma
9	Ryorinoma
10	Irori
11	Ido

N

Okiyodokoro

Honmaru Palace Complex

Valuable Remnants of Court Noble's Residence

Honmaru Palace is the castle's main enclosure, or Central Keep, which shogun Iyemitsu Tokugawa built in 1626. At the time it was composed of a castle tower five stories high and a palace compound of four buildings. Each of these burned to the ground, however, due to fire or lightning strikes. The manor we see here today was formerly the Katsura Imperial Family Palace within precincts of the Kyoto Imperial Palace, near Imadegawa Gate; it was moved here during the middle of the Meiji Period. A precious example of an Imperial Court residence, it is classified as an important cultural property. It consists of a drawing room, daily living quarters, kitchen and so on. Rising above a portion of the main tiled roof is a third-floor pavilion-like structure, giving the entire building a light and elegantly attractive appearance. While the main rooms of the first floor are done in typical shoin-zukuri style, those found on the third floor, by contrast, use lengthy log beams in a manner expressing a certain playful disregard for the conventions of Imperial court architecture. Many of the paintings found on the sliding panels and cedar doors within the former Katsura Imperial Family Palace were created by painters prolific during the late Edo and early Meiji periods.

本丸御殿

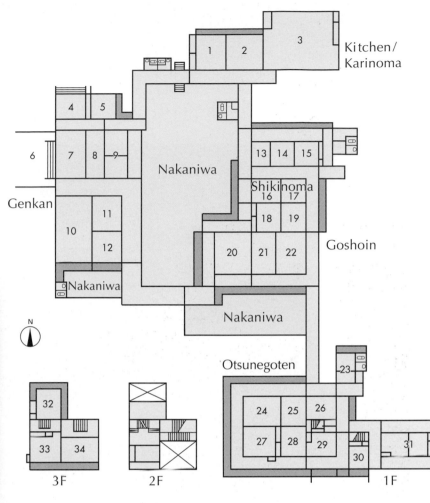

Kitchen/Karinoma

1 | 2 | 3

Nakaniwa

4 | 5

6 | 7 | 8 | 9

Genkan

10 | 11 | 12

Nakaniwa

13 | 14 | 15

Shikinoma
16 | 17
18 | 19

20 | 21 | 22

Goshoin

Nakaniwa

Otsunegoten

23

24 | 25 | 26
27 | 28 | 29
30 | 31

N

32
33 | 34

3F

2F

1F

1	Karinoma	13	Sannoma-kumo	25	Sannoma
2	Karinoma	14	Ninoma-tsuru	26	Gonoma
3	Daidokoro	15	Ichinoma	27	Ichinoma-gozanoma
4	Uchigenkan	16	Akinoma	28	Goshinjyo
5	Aosamuraibeya	17	Fuyunoma	29	Ladies' Waiting Room
6	Okurumayose	18	Harunoma	30	Keshounoma
7	Genkan	19	Natsunoma	31	Daichunoma
8	Torituginoma	20	Sannoma	32	Hikaenoma
9	Mendanjyo	21	Ninoma	33	Gozasho
10	Shishanoma	22	Ichinoma	34	Tsuginoma
11	Tenjyonoma	23	Yudono		
12	Kugyounoma	24	Ninoma		

Entryway

The entryway has been built facing west. The undulating bargeboard roof or Chinese gable of the porch gives way to the entrance hall and reception room. To the south is the envoy's room, and the corridor leads to the meeting room first on the left. On the right side are the courtier's room (Denjonoma) and court noble's room (Kugyohnoma). North of the entrance hall is an inner entrance hall.

Chushoin – Chamber of Four Seasons

Located on the north side of the Goshoin, these four utterly fascinating rooms are decorated with door panels depicting the four seasons. The room in the foreground is the summer room painted by Kyoshu Tamura, at back left is the main room or spring room by Oryu Maruyama, the back right is winter room by Sensui Hoshino, and to its left is the autumn room by Chikudo Kishi.

View of Ninoma (Second Room) and Ichinoma (First Room) from Sannoma (Third Room)

These rooms were used for formal audiences. The decorative molding of Ichinoma's raised floor is painted in black lacquer. The room has a raised alcove, staggered shelves and a coffered ceiling. The tatami mats of the Sannoma were taken out to convert this room into a Noh stage for plays to be performed for the Imperial family. The mannequins convey Imperial family customs and can be seen when this palace is open to the public on special occasions.

本丸御殿

本丸御殿

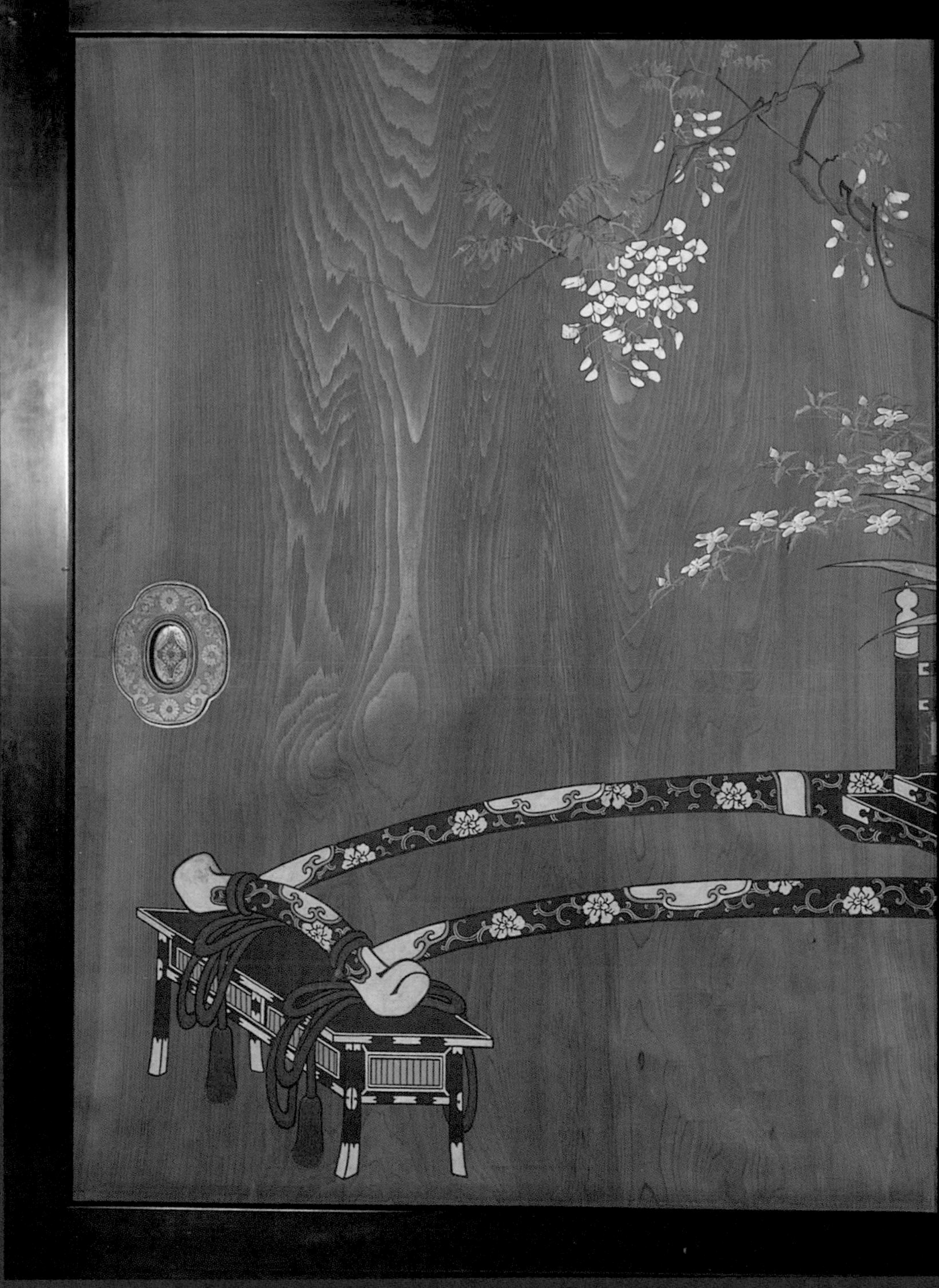

Flower Cart on Cedar Doors (facing out to corridor) of Kugyohnoma Chamber
 These are the first set of cedar doors acting as a partition to define the corridor passing from the entrance hall
(genkan) to Goshoin chamber. The beautiful flowered cart is appropriately regal and the peonies, hydrangeas
and chrysanthemums bedecking it are a vibrant delight to behold. The reverse sides of the doors are painted
with cranes and cherry trees. Both sides of the doors were painted by Kiho Yagi.

本丸御殿

External Appearance of Otsune Palace

Otsune palace, with its gently sloping roof, overlooks the even Honmaru garden, which was laid out when the palace was reconstructed here. The rear east wing, raised on an artificial mound, is a three-tier section, a sukiyaki style teahouse. From the third-floor vantage point, instead of looking down over the garden, ones gaze is held high on, and is seemingly returned by, the sentinel moon-viewing remains of the tower.

Pines and Cranes in Ichinoma, Otsune Palace

The pines and cranes painted by Eigaku Kano elegantly befit a noble's private chamber. This room has deep historical importance in that it was home to Emperor Komei's daughter princess Kazunomiya, the last Lady of the Katsura line of the Imperial family.

Turrets, Gates and Towers

Beautifully Decorated Karamon Gateway

The main entrance to Nijo Castle is the Higashi Otemon (Great East Gate) facing Horikawa Street. It is nearly 24 meters wide, with a pair of lookout turrets built into either side of a stone wall. These lookouts are two stories high and linked together; between and below them stands a fortified gate nine meters wide. It is believed that when Emperor Gomizuno-o visited here, this gate was converted into a single-story portal, then afterwards returned to its former contours. Gazing from the Great East Gate to the turret at the southeast corner, along the broad moat and immense stone wall stretching out to the south, one takes in a majestic scene fit for a castle.

As part of the structural reforms done in the Kan'ei era (1621-44) the tower of Fushimi Castle was transported to Nijo Castle and reconstructed in the Honmaru main enclosure. Another tower, which had stood within Ninomaru Palace at the time of the castle's foundation, was moved elsewhere. Of the main tower and eight other turrets only two turrets today remain.

Among the gates of Nijo Castle, the Karamon inner gateway to Ninomaru Palace is renowned for its splendor. The Chinese gables attached both front and back are elaborately sculpted and masterfully gilded.

Karamon Inner Gateway to Ninomaru Palace

This is the palace entrance built at the front of the Ninomaru palace. The undulating bargeboard or Chinese gable (karahafu) design is topped by a cypress bark roof and stands on four wooden posts (and two integral pillars) with beautifully carved and gilded eaves.

Great East Gate (top & left)

Here is Nijo Castle's front gate and the above shows it from a northeast angle. It is aligned with Nijo Street, an important road in the old capital. The sturdily built two-storey timber frame gatehouse has a metal-reinforced gateway set in the stone wall. The guard residence is above the gate as are stone dropping slits.

櫓と門

Western Gate (Uzumimon)

This is the castle's rear gate slotted into the stone wall and top wall. Though unassuming, this gate has a high inner embankment in the masugatai style that acts as a defense. Originally, this gate had a wooden bridge across the moat, and was normally the only means of entering and exiting the castle. This gate also is known as the farewell spot for the last shogun, Yoshinobu, who withdrew from power via this gate.

Southwest Corner Turret

A small but sturdy turret that afforded firm protection to the west. The undulating bargeboard gable on the second floor conveys the craftsmanship involved. Only short sections of the top wall remain either side of the turret, but originally they ran the circumference of the castle with stone dropping installations built in at strategic points. That long white wall supposedly looked like mist and thus Nijo was often called the "misty castle".

Southeast Corner Turret

This nestles in the southeast corner to the left of the Great East Gate. Two stories (both inner and outer) are stuccoed on the outside, with fortified retainers' residence windows on the first floor and bay windows on the both south and east sides that have stone dropping and archery slits. More retainers' residence windows can be seen on the second floor and triangular dormer gables (chidorihafu) decorate the south and north faces.

Rear View of Narukomon Gate

This is a gate to protect the northern end of the north/south drive between the Ninomaru and Honmaru Palaces. The front of the gate faces north and used to have a guardhouse on the outside.

Nagayamon Gate set in the Storehouses of Ninomaru

This is set in the storehouses in the northeast area of the kitchens. Originally, the storehouses stretched south to link up with a formal style fence or wall. The gate is the only significant one to provide entrance to Ninomaru palace from the north. To the left of the gate can be seen a built-in guardhouse, where the rambling writings of the guards remain.

Independent Raised Foundation and Inner Moat

This is the southwest corner of the stone-wall foundation protected by the inner moat. Standing approximately 15 meters high from waterline to top, it originally accommodated a five-story tower. The Emperor Gomizuno-o, leading figures and the shogun climbed this tower to enjoy the magnificent view of Kyoto.

Seiryuen Garden

清流園

Borrowing the vista of Honmaru's stone wall and timber frame gatehouse as a backdrop to the south, the magnificent Seiryuen Garden was landscaped in 1965. Originally occupied by billets for castle guards, this area became a garden during the Meiji period (1868 - 1912) and then a palace for Emperor Taisho's state ceremonies in the Taisho period (1912 - 1926).

View of Seiryuen Garden from Warakuan Teahouse

The babbling stream in front of the teahouse flows into a pond and off to the left can be seen Kountei arbor, which - a long with many of the garden stones - were moved here from the Suminokuraryoi mansion that used to stand on Kawaramachi and Nijo streets.

Warakuan Teahouse

This is modeled on the Omote Senke Zangetsutei arbor and is surrounded by a tea garden, which is full of variation. This and the rest of Seiryuen are used for tea parties for the public and entertaining national guests.

四季

春

Spring

This is the time of plum and cherry blossoms around the castle. With each change in this season, the blooms of trees like somei yoshino, yamazakara, shidarezakura and kurozakura can be enjoyed. With spring, Honmaru Palace is opened to the public and tea parties are held.

Summer

Along the south path of Seiryuen Garden can be seen the unusual tree shidare-enja that comes into bloom with tiny white "butterfly" flowers around the end of July.

夏

秋

Autumn

Once again in autumn the Honmaru Palace is opened to the public and tea parties are held. The Japanese bush clovers (hagi) discreetly flower and the trees take on their autumn hues, while a carpet of fallen leaves – notably the golden layer of ginkgo leaves – stretches out before the visitor.

Winter

Once or twice each winter, the lucky visitor can catch sight of the peaceful snow-draped palaces and gardens. The camellias in the castle grounds also can be seen in bloom from December to March.

冬

History of Conflict between Shogun and Emperor

Tokugawa Ieyasu, victorious in the Battle of Sekigahara in 1600, began building Nijo Castle in May of 1602. His purpose in creating this base in Kyoto was to mount a display of his power to the Emperor and to inhabitants of all the domains in Japan, making it clear that he had replaced Toyotomi Hideyoshi as lord of the realm. During this period Ieyasu normally resided in Fushimi Castle, but for political purposes more than for military strategy, he needed to build a residence near the Imperial Palace. It is certain that from the first he aimed to build a castle whose beauty and majesty surpassed Hideyoshi's Jurakudai. To initiate this project, the Ninomaru Palace portion of the castle was completed.

Soon afterwards, on March 27, 1603, an Imperial messenger was welcomed there for a great celebration of Ieyasu's installation as seiitaishogun (commander-in-chief of an expeditionary force against the barbarians). Moreover, for three continuous days beginning April 4th, Ieyasu invited royal courtiers and feudal lords to the castle for a grand party and sumptuous feast. Thus the historical drama known as the Tokugawa Shogunate was launched on the stage of this castle. Here, too, Ieyasu met with the son of Hideyoshi and subsequently made up his mind to destroy the Toyotomi family. Toward that end, the winter and summer sieges of Osaka Castle took place in 1614 and 1615, respectively, during which time Ieyasu's bakufu made their headquarters and directed military strategy from Nijo Castle. Much postwar business was also conducted here. During this time Ieyasu also invited court nobles and all persons concerned with Nijo Castle to attend his proclamation of a new code of laws confirming his de facto control over the Imperial Chrysanthemum Throne. Moreover, he issued regulations and prohibitions intended to severely restrict the authority of court nobles and religious figures such as priests. On the heels of these actions, Nijo Castle became the shogunate's central watchtower for observing, protecting and controlling the Imperial Court. Whenever the shogun came to Kyoto, the castle served as his lodgings. On its walls would be engraved the history of conflict between the Chrysanthemum and Hollyhock forces.

Years passed. Second-generation shogun Tokugawa Hidetada's daughter Kazuko came to serve as a court lady to Emperor Gomizuno-o, and a new palace was built in Nijo Castle to be used as her lodging house. As a result, to prepare for Emperor Gomizuno-o's pending visits, large-scale repairs and extensions were carried out in 1626 until the castle precincts reached their present scale: about 500 meters from east to west, and 400 meters from north to south. The Honmaru portion was added, more residential buildings erected, and the five-story tower from Fushimi Castle was reconstructed in the southwest corner. In connection with this, the aforementioned tower in Ninomaru Palace was moved to Yodo Castle. Moreover, the imperial guest house was built, and repairs and reconstruction were performed on the palaces and gardens. The military dictatorship further ordered that the Emperor's throne here must make use of ornate gold and silver. Kobori Enshu was among those nominated as magistrates in charge of construction. This building project and its burnishing of prestige was intended to show off to the world the power of the bakufu and its policy of public accommodation with the Imperial Court. The third-generation shogun Tokugawa Iemitsu and his father, the now-retired Hidetada, came to Kyoto to welcome the Emperor to the castle – the most glorious event in the history of Nijo Castle. The Emperor stayed for five days, and it is said that after seeing the many splendors of the castle he declared, " Now is the time of Maitreya. This is a heaven on earth." The Emperor also climbed the castle tower three times to enjoy its fine views of the capital.

Two hundred and sixty years after Ieyasu had built it, in March, 1863, the fourteenth-generation shogun Tokugawa Iemochi entered a dilapidated Nijo Castle: Its stately tower had been lost to a thunderbolt in 1750; the Honmaru palaces had burned down in the Kyoto's Great Fire of 1788. The castle was ruined, and the dazzling image of its former days was nowhere to be seen. The authority and capabilities of the military government had also declined. A rift arose between the Emperor and the government about the exclusion of foreigners from Japan, and a movement calling for the abolition of the bakufu was intensifying in the region of Choshu (present-day Yamaguchi Prefecture). Although Iemochi tried to achieve reconciliation between the Imperial Court and the bakufu, his efforts were in vain and he died with his hopes unrealized. Thus the torch was passed to the fifteenth-generation shogun Yoshinobu, who chose to assemble the feudal lords in Nijo Castle's Ohiroma in October, 1867 and declare the restoration of Imperial rule. And so it came to pass that the very same historic stage upon which the Tokugawa shogunate had celebrated its birth now became the site where its demise was proclaimed. The situation, however, was not settled merely by the shogunate surrendering authority to the throne. When Emperor Meiji visited Nijo Castle on February 3, 1868 (the first year of the Meiji era), he ordered the subjugation of the bakufu at an assembly held in the Shiro-shoin. The Tokugawa family suffered the dishonor of being declared criminals, while meantime, the anti-Tokugawa militia, led by Choshu and Satsuma (present-day Kagoshima Prefecture) marched towards Edo. Nijo Castle, which had served as the proud alter-ego of Edo Castle, was completely stripped of its functions and authority.

The buildings and grounds were requisitioned by the Imperial Court, and Imperial Representatives were stationed there. In 1872, the castle was transferred to the jurisdiction of the Kyoto Prefectural Office. Then, in 1885, jurisdiction was shifted to the Imperial Household Department, and the castle was renamed "Nijo Detached Palace." In 1894, the old palace of the Katsura Imperial family was relocated from the Kyoto Imperial Palace to the Central Keep (the present-day Honmaru Palace). Finally, in 1939, the site was donated to Kyoto City, which still owns it today. In 1994, Nijo Castle was registered as a world cultural heritage site based on the UNESCO World Heritage Convention, together with 17 other places, such as shrines and temples in Kyoto, Uji and Otsu.

Wall Paintings which Convey the Momoyama Fine Arts Style

The Ninomaru Palace buildings, which convey the essence of samurai architecture in early modern times, have well earned the title of national treasure with the grandeur of their brilliantly conceived interior structures and their elegant exteriors. In addition, the charm of the magnificent, luminous wall paintings in each of the rooms creates a very strong impression. These paintings cover not only the wall surfaces but the sliding panels and cedar doors to the outside as well, a style of decorating associated with the development of grand-scale castle architecture which prospered in the Momoyama era. Though it is certain that the wall paintings originally created for the Ninomaru Palace reached the pinnacle of fine arts in the Momoyama era, all of them were removed between 1624-26, during the repairs and renovation of the Kan'ei era, and we no longer know who painted them. The gold-and-jasper works which survive throughout the palace today were newly painted at the time of the renovation, using bright, opulent coloring and gold leaf in every chamber except for the Shiro-shoin private quarters. They were painted by artists of the Kano school, who regularly served as official painters for the bakufu military government. According to a tag attached to an old illustration of Nijo Castle, the paintings in Tozamurai were done by two Kano painters: Domi and Shinsetsu. Those in the Shikidai, Ohiroma and Sotetsunoma rooms were painted by Tanyu. Paintings in the Kuro-shoin are by Naonobu, and the works in the Shiro-shoin were created by Koi. These are the finest blooms of the early Kan'ei era, and speak to us of the style of the Momoyama period.

The History of Nijo Castle

1602	Shogun Ieyasu Tokugawa ordered all feudal lords of western Japan to construct Nijo Castle.
1603	Castle completed (parts of present Ninomaru Palace). Ieyasu visits and holds ceremony.
1611	Ieyasu tours castle with Hideyori Toyotomi (Ieyasu's rival).
1614	In December, Ieyasu leaves Nijo Castle with Hidetada (one of his sons) to wage war (Osaka Winter Campaign) on the Toyotomi clan.
1615	In May, Ieyasu sets out to attack Hideyori again (Osaka Summer Campaign). In July, in Nijo Castle, second Tokugawa shogun Hidetada promulgated the edict know as Kinchu Narabi Nikugesho Hatto, which was used to control the Imperial family and court nobles.
1620	Hidetada's daughter Kazuko (Tofukumonin) entered the castle as the wife of Emperor Gomizuno-o.
1624	Third shogun Iemitsu erects tower and Imperial reception palaces in readiness for Imperial visit.
1626	Honmaru, Ninomaru and tower completed and castle takes on present-day look.
	In September, Emperor Gomizuno-o and his wife Kazuko visit castle for five days.
	In this year, Tanyu Kano decoratively painted the door panels in the castle.
1634	Shogun Iemitsu proceeds to Kyoto and enters castle at the head of large army.
	From here on, guards known as zaiban (four leaders and 50 guards) were stationed at the castle.
1662	In May, a large earthquake caused serious damage to various locations within the castle (large statue of Buddha in Hokoji Temple destroyed).
1699	Castle administrator system ended and control maintained through two permanent leaders and ten horsemen and 20 lower-ranked patrolmen (feudal-era police).
1750	In August, the five-story tower was struck by lightening and destroyed by fire.
1788	In January, Honmaru complex and turrets destroyed in blaze that swept Kyoto (Tenmei conflagration).
1862	Construction commenced of facilities and temporary buildings for Ninomaru complex in readiness for visit to Kyoto by shogun Iemochi.
1863	Iemochi visits Nijo Castle as the first shogun since Iemitsu some 230 years earlier.
1866	Imperial proclamation handing shogunate to Yoshinobu Tokugawa takes place at the castle.
1867	In October, leaders of 40 feudal clans gather in the castle to hold a meeting to end the Edo Bakufu government and return power to the throne (taiseihokan).
	Yoshinobu handed power back to the throne in the Ohiroma chamber of the Ninomaru palace.
1868	In January, a Council of State (equivalent of modern-day Cabinet) was formed in Castle.
1871	Prefectural office located in Ninomaru palace, which later for a while came under the jurisdiction of the War Office.
1884	In July, castle becomes Imperial villa.
1893	Palace of Katsura Imperial family relocated from Kyoto Gosho Palace complex to Honmaru site to become Honmaru Palace. Relocation work completed in 1894 and Honmaru garden (lawns) developed.
1897	Ninomaru's bargeboards gilded and walls and ceilings of rooms and corridors decoratively painted.
1915	Banqueting hall (present-day Seiryuen garden) built for enthronement ceremony of Emperor Taisho.
	South gate completed.
1939	Imperial Household Ministry donates Nijo Imperial Villa (Nijo Castle) to Kyoto City.
1940	On February 11th, Nijo Castle opened to the public.
1952	In accordance with enactment of the Law for Protection of Cultural Properties, six constructions of Ninomaru palace designated as national treasures, and 22 constructions including Honmaru Palace and corner turrets designated important cultural properties.
1953	Ninomaru garden designated as special scenic spot.
1965	Seiryuen garden constructed (using stones and other items from the home of Ryoui Suminokura, a wealthy merchant of the early Edo period).
1982	Door panel paintings in Ninomaru palace designated important cultural properties.
	In April, preservation repair work commenced on Honmaru Palace.
1990	Preservation repair work completed on Honmaru Palace.
1994	Nijo Castle inscribed on World Heritage List.
2003	Celebrations held to commemorate the 400th anniversary of the castle.